The Purloined Letter

Fani Papageorgiou

The Purloined Letter

Shearsman Books

First published in the United Kingdom in 2017 by
Shearsman Books
50 Westons Hill Drive
Emersons Green
BRISTOL
BS16 7DF

Shearsman Books Ltd Registered Office
30–31 St. James Place, Mangotsfield, Bristol BS16 9JB
(this address not for correspondence)

www.shearsman.com

ISBN 978-1-84861-564-9

ACKNOWLEDGEMENTS
Some of the poems in this collection have previously appeared
in the following magazines:

No Need to Argue Anymore appeared in *The Baffler*

Boys vs. Girls appeared in
Free Verse: A Journal of Contemporary Poetry & Poetics

"The intellect suffers to pass unnoticed those consid-erations which are too obtrusively and too palpably self-evident."

— *Edgar Allan Poe*

To

Aris, Sophia, Ian,
Konstantinos & Artemis Stephanakis

Contents

Here is French chalk to mark cloth
the hollow in the ferns, the music on the platform,
our ten thousand interludes.

There is a smell of snow in the air
But still, acorns are alive.
We walk in the cold smelling of bonfires
Grinding the organ in the next town over
Looking for a dispatch on the other side of silence.

We do not retreat.
We do not get over it.
Ours is the remit of a king.

Sub rosa

The River Thames, 346 kilometres long,
flows West-East from Gloucestershire to the North Sea.
The word "Thames" comes from the Celtic "Tamesa"
meaning muddy and dark.

In the nineteenth century
steam ferries carried passengers along the Thames.
The ships' funnels lowered to fit beneath the bridges.
Now you don't see me, now you do.

It is a tidal river, its water partly fresh, partly salt.
Although the North Sea is 68 kilometres away,
one often hears seagulls in London.
You must not think we're unhappy.

Christopher Wren is buried in St. Paul's Cathedral.
On his tomb you read the inscription,
If you seek my monument, look around.
It is never enough to find another kingdom —
you must be able to hold it.

No one knows when ravens arrived at the Tower of London.
Since ancient times, the rose has been associated with secrecy.
Ceilings of dining rooms
have been decorated with carvings of roses,
to remind guests that what was said at the table
should be kept confidential,
a voice from a bottom of a well
a one-way street.

The wives of Henry VIII —
divorced, beheaded, deceased,
divorced, beheaded, survived.
The Tower always damp from the river.

Time will pass
you'll remember water
will seek other water
always downhill,
and though brackish water is half ocean, half rain
impurities can make water cleaner
cancelling your heart.
You're alive.

The Recurrence of Jefferson Davis

You were with your wife in the garden,
clipping roses,
when you heard the news of the presidency.
You had graduated from West Point and fought in Mexico.

There is a moment in any life
where you're standing in the middle of the sky.
You stay there
until that place no longer exists.

Then you spend your days thinking of lost causes
your blood sugar and water weight drained from your body.
Life is precarious.
There is and there isn't
through vessels delivering oxygen-rich blood
known as coronary arteries,
descending on the heart like a crown.
The Civil War was fought in the South.
You mourn for that sky until it chokes your heart.

You keep Confederate buttons in a box,
glory tucked away in the coves of your heart.
There is sunlight coming in from the French windows,
shiny squares of the room holding you in place.

There are stories of soldiers so weary
who could sleep while marching.

Not a single foreign nation
recognized the Confederate States of America.
These were the complicated years.

Like the sign at the Baptist church —
WHOEVER IS PRAYING FOR RAIN, PLEASE STOP.

Seagulls

1.
We have no peace.

2.
We can tell you how we walk around twenty miles a day.
How the clean wind is blowing on the coast.
How it is not possible to measure pleasure.

3.
We walk along the coast every day
and the trees tell us we will have a long life.

4.
We spend time losing things.
Poplars look like ghosts.
We will take away everything you have, they whisper.
How they have tormented us.

5.
There is a terrible racket in our heads.
If we do harm by walking into a darkening garden,
what is it about the pain of others?

6.
We're ravenous here.
Can't you see.
Walking is not about shedding burdens.

7.
On the train from Paddington to St. Austell,
reaching the South Coast,
we could see the tides from the window
small dinghies on the sand.
Life is like that.

8.
Connect these dots:
National Trust, wooden gates bleached by the sun,
seaweed and driftwood on a beach,
fields with muck by the ocean, sea air,
church, tombstones, palm trees.

9.
We eat Cornish oysters freshly plucked from their beds.
There is a storm outside the French windows
and for a minute it feels as if response
is the most profound measurement of consciousness.

10.
We get scalded when we brush our teeth.
Always different taps in England for cold and hot.
No matter how fast we run our hands under them,
we can never have both.

11.
Behind our breastbones,
the air from the Atlantic sweeping everything away.
Do you know me, it says.

12.
Matthew Arnold said,
I *really* believe that life is *long* —
long enough to contain everything —

13.
If seagulls are the souls of dead sailors
crying that love slows you down
no one is listening.

14.
A very serious lack of vitamin B1 causes a disease called beriberi.
In Sinhalese, beriberi means "I cannot, I cannot",
and refers to the fact that sufferers have difficulty walking
due to nerve damage and muscle atrophy.

15.
We wonder if we have made a terrible mistake.
We can stand in Dover and wave to people in Calais.
There are seagulls warning us not to expect anything back.

16.
The Waiting Room – blue distances in the evening sunset.
It will blot out everything.

17.
We can squander it all.
They say alcohol was invented
because otherwise the Irish would conquer the world.

18.
The Phoenicians were seafarers,
they carried language around
and as a result the vowels changed.
The word *alone* started as all-one.
An inmate in a maximum-security prison in Kansas said,
*Can you imagine not being able to touch another human being
for twenty-three fucking years?*

19.
Matthew Arnold was elected
Professor of Poetry at Oxford in 1857.
He was the first in his position
to deliver his lectures in English, rather than in Latin.
In 1861 he delivered three lectures titled *On Translating Homer*.
The way miners use dynamite to bleed a vein,
Arnold gives practical advice
and the lectures become backlit stained glass,
imprints from the sun.
He advises the translator to have nothing to do
with the question of whether Homer existed
and whether the poet of the *Iliad* was one or many.

20.
Agamemnon has a dream that tells him he will take Troy.
Some things cannot be faced head on.
Giddy comes from God is inside you.

21.
In his lectures, Arnold states again and again
that any translator of Homer should be imbued
with the four qualities which characterize the author:
He is eminently rapid.
He is eminently plain and direct both in his syntax and his words.
He is eminently plain and direct in the substance of his thought,
that is, in his matter and ideas.
He is eminently noble.

22.
If I throw a nickel inside you,
it will keep travelling
and I won't hear the click straight away.
The woods go on for hundreds of miles.

23.
Arnold goes on to analyse each existing translation
explaining why it doesn't work.
He identifies the qualities lacking.
On the version of the *Iliad* by Alexander Pope,
he quotes Bentley, *You must not call it Homer.*

24.
Try to remember.
Try hard.
What do the seagulls say before diving into the water.

25.
Pope's style is so bad mainly because it is pompous and artificial.
Chapman's version is better but too Elizabethan.
Keats had fallen in love with Chapman's Homer
but Keats could not read the original,
as he did not know Ancient Greek.

26.
We can no longer stay in our heads.
We have no peace
A zigzag across our hearts.

27.
How shall it end now?
Asks Jupiter to Juno in the final lines of *The Aeneid.*
Believing things doesn't make them true.
The sound of an armour when a man is felled.
The grid of streets in a modern city.

28.
In *The Iliad* the Greeks are a long way from home.
Two hundred and sixty four people die in the course of the book.
Bronze, a mixture of tin and copper,
dark brown and shiny, turns green as it gets older.

29.
Homer, Arnold tells us,
expresses himself like a man of adult reason.
He is unrivalled in the clearness
and straightforwardness of his thinking.

30.
The morning is clear and blue.
You must be complex to want simplicity.

31.
Arnold demonstrates how all the translators fail to render Homer
by quoting specific passages from *The Iliad.*
He chooses the passage at the end of the nineteenth book,
where Achilles answers his horse Xanthus,
who has prophesied his death to him,
after the death of Patroclus.
He shows how Chapman's manner and movement
are un-Homeric.
Homer is always simple and intelligible.
He is neither quaint nor antiquated.
His manner invests his subject,
whatever his subject [may] be,
with nobleness.

32.
Arnold closes his third lecture telling us that
Homer has the liquid clearness of an Ionian sky.
Remember.
The Greeks camped on the end of the beach.
The calm that spreads across the sea.
What is the point of a risk free life?

33.
The English Channel is filled with very cold water,
strong tides and stronger currents.
Four hundred yards off the English coast,
we can see the white cliffs of Dover
the pebbles on the beach.

34.
Homer's rapidity is a flowing rapidity.
Arnold argues that is the essence of Homer's style,
his sustained nobility,
which can form the character as it is edifying.
In the twenty-four books of *The Iliad*,
there is no description of Helen.

35.
Try to remember.
The Christian doctrine of the Atonement
has been foreshadowed in the *Iliad*
Only meandering allows that.

36.
The Touch of Death is a martial technique so advanced
that with a simple touch to an unspecified part of the body,
it can reverse the vital mechanism and bring about death
within twenty-four hours.
Life is full of people who wait.

37.

We never know exactly what the fighting is about.
Once again the Trojans drive the Greeks back to their ships.

38.

Exhaustion takes so much out of people,
but never everything.
A fisherman is buried with his line and net.
Is *The Iliad* an ancient guidebook to the stars?

39.

Matteo Ricci conveyed to the Ming court
that China might not be the Middle Kingdom,
that other large countries exist,
that the earth is round.

40.

An early bicycle was invented
when the Year Without Summer
pushed the cost of grain and hay beyond reach
and rendered horses unaffordable.

41.

Nelson's body was preserved in a cask of brandy
before it reached St. Paul's.
At Gibraltar, the brandy was changed to spirits,
as seagulls were crying overhead.

42.
We do not have Ruth's letters to Mallory
during the Everest expeditions.

43.
When Dutch explorers landed on Easter Island in 1722
they met a Stone Age culture.
Archaeologists cannot explain the ability
to carry giant statues upright across miles of uneven terrain.
The statues walked, Easter Islanders said.

44.
The sandwiches are eaten, the blanket is folded,
the tide has ebbed, the day is over.
Seagulls walking on the rim of the seawall.
Everywhere, the world is the same.

45.
The International Flat Earth Society
has approximately 3,500 members.
A seagull murmur to evoke the eddy in the heart.

46.
Throw a dead animal, such as a goat or sheep,
into the water downstream from where you want to cross.
The carcass will attract the piranhas
and give you some time to cross, but not much.

47.
Before chronometers were invented,
clocks had pendulums
but they didn't work on ships.
How much blood can you lose
before you bleed to death?

48.
It is often an unfortunate event,
which proves decisive
in shaping a life towards better things.
In 424 B.C. Thucydides failed as a general
leading the Athenians in the Peloponnesian War
to save Amphipolis from Vrasidas
and was therefore exiled.
His country lost a mediocre general
while humanity gained a great historian.
Experience is not transferable.

49.
Don Quixote makes himself a helmet from the pages of a book.
He tests the helmet and, when it breaks,
he satisfies himself by choosing not to test it a second time.

50.
Connect these dots:
the white dish towels drying on the rack,
eyeless salamanders pausing at the mouth of a cave,
something else but not life.

51.
There was a crack in the concrete wall of the garage,
when we were growing up,
and we used to squeeze ourselves inside.

52.
I cannot, I cannot,
Where is the love without the risk,
the life that gestures towards repair.
How far does the nickel travel inside you
Where do you have to stand to see the white cliffs of Dover
Why is everything foreshadowed in the *Iliad*
Why do so many people die in the course of that book

53.
Why do we behave differently at night
Why did the use of candles spread with the advent of sash windows
What does the Waiting Room mean
Where do you have to stand to wave at people at Calais
Why are we all so ravenous
Why are seagulls always crying
What else is there but wasting it all
Do seas provide salt and cement?
Do we ever hear music through a doorway?

54.
We close our eyes.
During the Civil War,
soldiers had their legs amputated
with only sips of rye whiskey.
We open our eyes.

55.
Every human being walks.
Help is on the way.
A glassy sea, a ceramic blue sky.

56.
There is no tourniquet, cry the seagulls.
All the king's horses and all the king's men
won't fix the laced bones of your spine,
your derelict heart.
Connect the dots, we tell them,
make some sense of all this
I cannot, I cannot.

The Delta

1.
You land at Democritus International Airport
early in the morning.
The sea, smooth as glass,
has outlived everything that defines it.

2.
This is the hour of light.
A man resting in shade
in one-hundred-degree temperatures
loses a cup of water an hour —
the slowest rate of water loss
possible in such heat.

3.
A man marching in such conditions
loses two quarts of water an hour,
expending his water reserves eight times as quickly.

4.
Tell me things.
You know something.
You have found it in your sleep.

5.

The statisticians have shown us
how much can be learned
by counting the dead
but who wants to stop walking.

6.

You spend hours staring at the lighthouse in the port
from your room on the top floor of *Park Hotel*,
a red flapping tent on its balcony.
Life means abrupt losses of meaning.

7.

You're carrying the *Letters of Flannery O'Connor*
and *Lady's Chatterley's Lover*
from café to café.
D.H. Lawrence said
one sheds one's sickness in books.

8.

In 1920, the King of Greece, Alexander I, visited the city
and the authorities decided to name it in his honour.
You can't pin things down without changing them.
Is the story we tell in our heads the most important one?

9.
Flannery O'Connor lived on a dairy farm, *Andalusia*,
with her mother, Regina.
She believed that, "vocation implies limitation"
and in the notion of "passive diminishment" —
the serene acceptance of whatever affliction or loss
cannot be changed by any means.
Can one live and write at the same time?

10.
After a few months at sea,
the sun bleaches the mind
one starts to see what one wishes to see.
Waiting muffles the world.
Tell me what I need to know.

11.
The Treaty of Lausanne in 1923 affirmed
that Western Thrace and Alexandroupolis
would continue to be controlled by Greece.
The iron railing on the seafront,
slowly rusting in the corrosive salt air.

12.
According to the plaque
the lighthouse functioned for the first time on June 1st 1880.
Height from sea level: 27 meters
Height from the ground: 17 meters
Scope of light band: 24 nautical miles
Show me a village and I'll show you the world.

13.
Boys chasing girls around the yard during recess.
Objects in mirror are closer than they appear.

14.
What you feel is the quickening.
The Danube River has a different name
in every country it flows through.
I may forget myself and push you overboard.

15.
This is the hour of darkness.
You walk along the promenade,
a ribbon on the Thracian Sea,
the menu in the tavernas in Greek and Bulgarian.
During World War II
the Nazis gave Alexandroupolis
to their Bulgarian partners.

16.
Boys vs. Girls.
Iron is permeable to magnetic force.

17.
This is the hour of bedbugs.
Who has ever slowed his own heart?

18.
Somewhere a car smashes into a tree.
Each and every adventure serves one purpose —
that one day, peace will be enough.

19.
Alexandroupolis was only a fishing village
until the late 19th century.
You're nine miles west from the river Evros.
Memory is not the carcass of a whale
on the ramp of an old port.

20.
Another day down.
The shafted windows, the sky.
The surface of a puddle of water
at the foot of the Himalaya
will assume an irregular form
because of the gravitational pull.
Between pain and nothing,
which one would you choose?

21.
Once lived a man called Baron Münchausen
who travelled all over Germany,
from town to town,
faking illness.
The world is full of people who can write only one story
wrote Flannery O'Connor in a letter.

22.
They say that there have been many Ice Ages.
That spirits can tap into electric currents,
that in your writing
you can make love to whomever you want.

23.
Evros Delta is a coastal wetland,
a mix of fresh, brackish and salt waters
the shallow waters ideal for waterfowl and waders.
*"I would like to have all the rest of the world disappear
and live with you here,"* Lady Chatterley told her lover.
"It won't disappear," he said.

24.
As the days are getting colder
a shuffle of yellow leaves appears on our porches
we think that maybe winter is coming,
that we should draught-proof the windows,
stop up the doors.

25.
What to do with happiness.
Without the protection of pain,
limbs get damaged.
Without carbon, there is no life.

26.
The buttercup is the prevailing floating plant in the Delta.
If you walk through the marshes,
you'll reach a sandy beach
oystercatchers and plovers stealing themselves into your dreams.

27.
Cormorants are the best fishermen
being so close to the Dardanelles,
the second biggest bottleneck of migration
in southeastern Europe.
The earth beneath you is turning.

28. ·
Evros Delta was submitted to pressure
due to the irrigation projects in the 1950s.
The first rule of Fight Club —
don't talk about Fight Club.

29.
The flamingos are dusty pink
because of the gambari shrimp they eat.
The light on your hands diaphanous and precise
the belief that life is somehow reparable.

30.
Two ladies are sharing a railway compartment —
I don't believe in ghosts, says one to the other.
Oh, really? The other replies and vanishes.

31.
You walk like Odysseus's crewmate, Elpenor,
who had fallen off the roof of Circe's house,
being so happy he had forgotten
he had to use a ladder to come down.
Is one man, all men?

32.
You sit on a bench opposite the island of Samothrace
its contours shimmering in the silver blue light.
There's nothing coherent in upheaval.
Must one be calm twenty-four hours a day?

33.
There the light fails more quickly,
like a live wire.
They say nothing prepares you
for the evening creeping in.
You could see why strangers
came for gas and stayed forever.

34.
A circle hasn't any corners.
A whispering gallery is a hemispherical enclosure
beneath a dome or a vault
in which whispers can be heard clearly
in other parts of the gallery.

35.
In November 1949,
Flannery O'Connor wrote a letter to her friend Betty Boyd
who had just announced her engagement.
O'Connor is awkward in her efforts
to respond to such happy news.
She has chosen special paper to write on,
to honour the occasion
(white, 16-pound bond).

36.
She asks her friend
if she intends to live in Los Angeles
where her fiancé is based
and finally she says
she would like to send her a teaspoon
as a wedding gift.
What kind would you like me to send?

37.
She leaves a large space at the bottom
to make the letter look more nuptial.
But then she doesn't sign off
with the standard salutations —
best wishes, love — but with
An abundance of peace.

38.
In the Sahara,
the palaces of rulers were constructed in such a way
as to maximize cross ventilation
but in Antarctica the danger for humans
is chiefly the wind.

39.
The term *spinster* originated in fifteenth-century Europe
to describe the girls who spun thread for a living.
These girls were usually unmarried
so the term became synonymous with the *old maid*.

40.
Since only wives were allowed to have sex,
these women were scorned
for the experiences they never had.
Can one live and write at the same time?

41.
Evros is the biggest river in the Balkans,
the natural border between Greece and Turkey.
If you tap on the glass, will the ghosts go away?

42.
You have learned the low and high tides by heart
for every day of the calendar,
You know salt keeps things clean
everything there is to know about stain removal.

43.
People who lie, do so about love.
It is not hard to imagine things the other way around.
When they asked kindergarteners in Geneva
they said Lac Léman
had been dug deliberately after the city was built
by men with spades.

44.
In whispering galleries,
sound carries along the curve of the wall
on the rim of the dome.
The sea is never infinite —
There's always land on the other side.

45.
Pluto was demoted to a dwarf planet.
Girls standing in the middle of the highway,
on the dividing line.
Time went on as the clock does,
half past eight instead of half past seven,
as Lady Chatterley is waiting to see her lover.

46.
A piece of you is turning towards the sun.
One, two, three, four —
we declare a thumb war.

47.
The dream in which
there is a stranger in your kitchen,
his eyes steady and clear.
Any story I reveal myself completely in will be a bad story,
writes O'Connor in her letters.

48.
Life is to be approached with waltzing moves
towards the place we experience disorder.
Like you, I hide in plain sight.

49.
Happiness is harder on the lungs
light fades
and you must not touch any hallowed things.

50.
Yet even the sun looks wrong —
its taffeta gleam a dark patch
blooming across the ceiling.
Anything can be anywhere.

51.
The entire Delta is a military zone,
people smuggling cigarettes across borders.
So I love chastity now,
because it is the peace that comes of fucking
Lawrence writes in his novel.
Can one live and write at the same time?

52.
How to safely unearth a young tree
from one corner of your backyard
and move it to another, one that got more sun.
Boys vs. Girls.
The belief that life is somehow reparable.

53.
Nothing can happen to you that you can't use.
Cartographers call the blank spaces on maps,
sleeping beauties.

54.
They say the city was given its name
in honour of Alexander the Great
who once crossed it
while leading Greek troops to Andrianoupolis.
Life is throwing matches into the sidewalk gutters
where the wastewater runs,
then following the course of those matches.

55.
Lady Gwendolen Cecil
used up her old evening dresses
by gardening in them.
To live deliberately.
Remembering is half of life.
Talk to me.

56.
Imagine the Aegean drained away.
Whatever is wet escapes burning.

57.
Alexandroupolis connects Europe and Asia
in 1897 the Orient Express reached the city.
A motel facing the interstate.
You vs. the whoosh of the passing cars —
like living by the sea.

58.
So will you stand next to me
for the next twenty minutes?
I keep losing —
I need my luck turned around.

59.
And then there are the animals
pictured on the walls in Lascaux,
the cracks of your own heart.

60.
Bays and rivers are named.
Fragments of harpoons
are still found in the desert.
How to live.

61.
Greek towns smelling of *Tide*.
The rustle of things migrating to the brain,
guiding us as we move through labyrinths.

62.
There are things that won't leave us alone,
canisters from old British army supplies,
that never disappear.

63.
Must one be calm twenty-four hours a day?
We take sexual energy
and aim it somewhere else.

64.
Life means abrupt losses of meaning.
After a few months at sea,
one starts to see what one wishes to see.
Sleeping beauties muffle the world.

65.
Our plans for wild happiness.
Anthropologists report
even trepanned skulls show signs of healing.

66.
Objects in mirror are closer than they appear.
The tides troubled Captain Vancouver the most.
He named the water, Desolation Sound.

67.
The sea is out to kill us.
You can't make yourself want
what you don't want.
There is a wind in North Africa,
whose dust causes giddiness.

68.
Girls embroidering butterflies
onto the edges of tea towels.
What does a broken heart mean
if we know emotion stems from the brain?

69.
Boys chasing girls
around the yard during recess.
How ravished one could be
without ever being touched

70.
Afternoon sunlight
on the blue windows of buses and cars.
Boys gathering on bridges
hurling rocks on trains passing by.

71.
To love a man is to fly behind enemy lines,
rescuing downed pilots.
To start a journey in a sandstorm
is good luck.

72.
Quantum weirdness refers to the fact
that an observed particle behaves very differently
from one that is unobserved.
Falling glass will break
unless you catch it.

73.
Ash can even preserve the imprint of raindrops.
There are no clean starts.
For whom was Alexandroupolis named?

74.
You can attenuate wire by drawing it
through smaller and smaller holes
if there's a kind of singing that goes in your head.

75.
Storms sift and grade the size of shingle
trepanned skulls show signs of healing
time alone gives definition.

76.
In Latin *norma* means *square*, the carpenter's square.
Until the 1830s the English word *normal*
meant standing at a right angle to the ground.
Who has ever slowed his own heart?

77.
Spilling a full teacup over a linen tablecloth.
When you're young,
your lungs have a huge reserve capacity —
You will have an arduous life,
they whisper.

78.
We can be wrong or we can know it
but we can't do both at the same time.
Kalashnikov said, *I wish I had invented a lawnmower.*

79.
People only speak to get something.
The ghastly wanting
a snowstorm in a Victorian paperweight.

80.
Somewhere a car smashes into a tree.
It's not easy to hurt the central nervous system.
Is the story we tell in our heads the most important one?

81.
Another day down.
The shafted windows, the sky.
A woollen mill produces yarn, flannel and blankets
love happens in the head.

82.
Cantor's definition of infinity,
a hotel with endless rooms.
Have you ever had a tune caught in your head?

83.
Ptolemy was right.
The Nile does flow
from a great lake in the middle of Africa.

84.
In 1984 two small clay tablets
of vaguely rectangular shape
were found in Tell Brak, Syria,
dating from the fourth millennium B.C.
and this is the oldest sample of writing we know.

85.
One thing smoke does is lower your voice.
Sticks and stones will break your bones,
not everything will pass.

86.
Jasper Johns said,
what if the traffic light said RUN
or RUN FOR YOUR LIFE.

87.
The mind is a little town
with a river running through.
A mole does not come from the skin itself
but from the central nervous system.

88.
Upon reaching Assisi,
Nikos Kazantzakis was so elated
that he had to wear his shoes one size smaller
to bear the happiness.
Some shoes take you anywhere but home.

89.
Whisper along the curving wall —
there have been many Ice Ages,
spirits can tap into electric currents,
in your writing
you can make love to whomever you want.

90.
Ask me one more time and I'll tell you.
You need a knife you can trust.

91.
Here's the church,
Here's the steeple.
Open it up,
Where are the people?

92.
Well, so many words, because I can't touch you.
In the morning, you water the roses
before the fog burns off.

93.
Two women who shared a cell for twenty-five years
were released on the same day,
and stood outside the prison gate
talking for an hour.

94.
Cross my heart —
Here.
The people are here.

95.
In the Sahara,
the palaces of rulers were constructed in such a way
as to maximize cross ventilation
but in Antarctica
the danger for humans is chiefly the wind.
We've got to live,
no matter how many skies have fallen.

96.
The holding back —
a refraction of light from oil slick, soap bubbles, fish scales.
Cairns guiding travellers.
The puddles.

97.
The statisticians have shown us
how much can be learned by counting the dead
but who can live and write at the same time
who wants to stop walking.

98.
The oceans will wear away our coasts,
soon we'll be walking on stilts.
Still, we have coffee and books,
we have ramparts built on sand
we have this life.

The Light in the Hallway

The sun is a hammer
but there are still shadows and places to hide
the air smelling of hot leaves and diesel
boys somewhere diving off a wharf.

You arrive in the beginning of August,
dragging your suitcase up the steep stairs
of the prewar brownstone, to the rent-controlled apartment
leased to a Greek banker far away
travelling the world.

You do push-ups until you see black dots.
This is not the time for sleeping.
Do girls have all the fun?
You bleach the counters and scrub the floors,
your head a car crashing into telephone poles.

There are bay windows,
a fireplace in the bedroom,
a deck lined with plants.
Your job is to inhabit the property
and water the plants, special emphasis on the ficus.

In the blue afternoon shadows you sit still,
watching the men playing chess in Washington Square.
If you open a manhole on the sidewalk,
will you see the North Atlantic, you wonder.

At night you lie on the sofa, book propped on cushions
wine glass, pretzels and cigarettes
scattered on the coffee table next to the fresh oregano
your mother has sent from Greece.
Do astronauts still go to the moon?

You know no one in the city.
Astronauts in space worry about their bone density
in the absence of gravity.

You read with no purpose and no goal in sight
except to discover what other people think —
their heart at the moment it breaks.

The cleaning lady drops by to hand you her keys.
Her name is Beata, you have coffee in the kitchen.
She is moving from Greenpoint back to Warsaw.
After the war, Poland becomes Communist country —
Eastern Bloc, you see?
Beata tells you.
How would I not know this?

The heart is prone to sinking.
This is how life will always be.
Your weight towards the centre of the earth,
crushing your chest.

You hug Beata in the doorway,
wishing each other good luck.
You will never see her again.
Why are manhole covers round?

The curtains are drawn but the bright afternoon leaks in.
You can't sit in the sun but you get shivers in the shade.
First rule of life as an adventure, leave home.
If you paid attention to the advice and the warnings,
you'd never go anywhere.

You bleach the counters and scrub the floors,
your head a car crashing into a tree.

In February 1945, at the Yalta Conference,
it was decided that Poland would remain under Soviet control.
Perhaps, you think this does not apply to you.

You use your hands to make shapes and shadows on the glass.
There are spots on the wall from water damage,
a Ferris wheel in the distance.
Good luck Beata.

The brain is a mass of blood vessels.
Portals pop up in the oddest places —
forests, stones, pictures of boats.
Blink and you may miss it
but you do, in order to find life.

Here is French chalk to mark cloth
the hollow in the ferns, the music on the platform,
our ten thousand interludes.

There is a smell of snow in the air
But still, acorns are alive.
We walk in the cold smelling of bonfires
Grinding the organ in the next town over
Looking for a dispatch on the other side of silence.

We do not retreat.
We do not get over it.
Ours is the remit of a king.

Sources

"The world is full of people who can write only one story.
Any story I reveal myself completely in will be a bad story."

The Letters of Flannery O'Connor, *The Habit of Being*,
selected and edited by Sally Fitzgerald,
Farrar, Straus & Giroux, New York, 1979

"Well, so many words, because I can't touch you"

"I would like to have all the rest of the world disappear," she said,
"and live with you here." "It won't disappear," he said.

"We've got to live, no matter how many skies have fallen."

"So I love chastity now, because it is the peace that comes of fucking."

"Time went on as the clock does, half past eight instead of half past
seven."

D.H. Lawrence, *Lady Chatterley's Lover*,
Penguin, London 1963

www.ingramcontent.com/pod-product-compliance
Lightning Source LLC
Chambersburg PA
CBHW031934080426
42734CB00007B/682